African-American Soldiers

The 761st Tank Battalion

Kathryn Browne Pfeifer

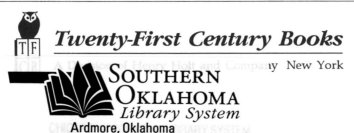

Twenty-First Century Books

A Division of Henry Holt and Company New York

PHOTO CREDITS

cover: flag by Fred J. Eckert/FPG International; photo courtesy of U.S. Army Military History Institute. **4:** U.S. Army photo courtesy of the Patton Museum, Fort Knox, KY. **9:** Courtesy of E. G. McConnell. **19:** UPI/Bettmann. **23:** E. G. McConnell. **27:** Patton Museum. **28:** NYPL/Schomburg Center for Research in Black Culture. **33:** AP/Wide World. **39, 43, 46, 56:** Patton Museum. **64:** Library of Congress. **66:** Bart Bartholemew/The New York Times. **71:** U.S. Army Military History Institute. **73:** E. G. McConnell. **75:** Patton Museum.

The map on page 68 is by Patricia Tobin

Twenty-First Century Books
A Division of Henry Holt and Company, Inc.
115 West 18th Street
New York, NY   10011

Henry Holt® and colophon are trademarks of
Henry Holt and Company, Inc.
Publishers since 1866

Published in Canada by Fitzhenry & Whiteside Ltd.,
195 Allstate Parkway
Markham, Ontario   L3R 2T8

Library of Congress Cataloging-in-Publication Data

Pfeifer, Kathryn Browne.
The 761st Tank Battalion / Kathryn Browne Pfeifer. — 1st ed.
p.   cm. — (African-American soldiers)
Includes bibliographical references and index.
1. United States. Army. Tank Battalion, 761st—History.
2. World War, 1939-1945—Regimental histories—United States.
3. United States. Army—Afro-American troops—History—20th century.
I. Title. II. Series.
D769.306 761st.P44   1994
940.54'1273—dc20   93-45799   CIP

ISBN 0-8050-3057-3
First edition—1994

Printed in Mexico
All first editions are printed on acid-free paper ∞.

10 9 8 7 6 5 4 3 2 1

Contents

Chapter 1

Come Out Fighting

Heavy snow covered the trees, rooftops, and rutted roads of the small Belgian village of Gerimont. It was early January 1945, and the scene looked like a picture postcard. But to the soldiers meeting inside one of the village houses, the scene outside was anything but beautiful. They knew that German tank destroyers were lurking in the forested hills to the north. The view to the east didn't look any brighter: the hillside leading down to the German-occupied town of Tillet was strewn with disabled American tanks. The orders the men had received earlier that day—to take the town of Tillet—seemed impossible to carry out. To the man in charge of ensuring that the orders were fulfilled, the burden of responsibility seemed too great to assume alone.

Captain David J. Williams, commander of Able Company, 761st Tank Battalion, had called his sergeants together for the meeting. He knew the waiting game he and his men were playing

A private guards the snow-covered tanks of the 761st Tank Battalion with the Germans could not last much longer. The Germans had been trying for several days to get the Americans to fight, provoking them with mortar fire. The enemy had even sent some of their infantry, camouflaged in white sheets, up the hillside from Tillet in an attempt to engage Williams and his men in battle. Although the Americans were returning fire and had even gone as far as faking an attack on the Germans, Williams had been reluctant to completely commit his men to battle. He was waiting for reinforcements, for he had been told that the 17th Airborne would be joining them any day. However, time appeared to be running out. To make matters worse, the infantry division Able Company had been assigned to was young and inexperienced, which greatly worried Captain Williams and his men.

Williams leveled with his sergeants: "If the Germans . . . attack us, we can't hold them, and I guarantee you that if we resist, they'll kill us all. Now I'm the company commander, but I'm going to bow out of this one. This is one decision you guys have got to make. Do you want me to wave my underwear or do you want to fight it out?"

Sergeant Walter Lewis spoke up immediately. "We can't give up, Captain," he said softly. "It wouldn't be right. I say we fight it out." The room filled with laughter. Lewis was such a quiet fellow;

he was the last person that anyone thought would speak up. However, the others agreed with him. Someone said, "If Walter wants to fight it out, then we'll fight it out." The meeting adjourned.

Elsewhere in the area, the other companies of the 761st Tank Battalion—Baker, Charlie, Dog, Service, and Headquarters—were tackling their own problems. The cold weather and slippery terrain made it practically impossible for the trucks of Service Company to reach the front lines with new supplies of ammunition, so the light tanks of Dog Company stepped in and took over those operations. The other two combat companies— Baker and Charlie—found the German resistance in the area of Tillet tougher than they expected; the men knew that they would have to fight viciously for every inch of ground. This was the Battle of the Bulge, one of Germany's last, desperate attempts to split the Allied forces and gain control of Belgium.

The 761st Tank Battalion had been in Europe since October 10, 1944. General George S. Patton of the Third United States Army had needed replacement tankers and wanted only the best left in the United States, so the 761st was sent to him. When the battalion reached France, it had the distinction of being the first African-American armored unit to be committed to combat in World

War II. Only six men attached to the battalion were white; they were all officers, and Captain David Williams was among them.

Although small in size, the 761st Tank Battalion proved early on that, indeed, it was one of United States Army's best tank outfits. The men of the battalion not only fought like their mascot the black panther, but they also lived up to their motto: "Come out fighting!" Their record is impressive, especially considering how the army used tank battalions.

"The average life of a separate tank battalion," explained Charles A. Gates, former commander of Charlie Company, "was from ten to twelve days. When there was a bad spot, they'd send the separate tank battalion in the area . . . . You were just gun fodder really." Yet the 761st proved they were more than gun fodder, staying in combat for 183 consecutive days—a record few, if any, other army units during World War II could match.

The battalion had entered the war at six o'clock on the morning of November 8, 1944, at Athainville, France, fifty miles from the German border. Attached to the United States 26th Infantry Division, the unit had received instructions to send out two task forces along an eleven-mile front and "sweep everything before them, converge, and funnel their way into the heart of the enemy's stoutest defenses." By the end of the day, the battalion had taken three towns and one hill away from the enemy, but it paid the price in casualties. Six enlisted men died and two officers were wounded, including the battalion's leader, Lieutenant Colonel Paul L. Bates. The men of the 761st had gotten their first taste of battle. Any initial fear or tension the men had felt that morning had been wiped away and replaced with a stubborn determination to rout the enemy from its positions.

Lieutenant Colonel Paul L. Bates

Heavy fighting continued the next day as snow began to fall, helping to camouflage enemy tanks and artillery. But their years of training began to pay off for the men of the 761st. Town after town fell into their hands, and they reached the German border by December 14.

Major General Manton S. Eddy, commander of the XII Corps of the United States Army (under whose authority the 26th Infantry Division fell), praised the unit's success, noting that "the 761st Tank Battalion [has] entered combat with such conspicuous courage and success." He wrote, "The speed with which they adapted themselves to the front line under most adverse weather conditions, the gallantry with which they faced some of Germany's finest troops, and the confident spirit with which they emerged from their recent engagements . . . entitle them surely to consider themselves the veteran 761st."

From the German border, Patton's now seasoned tankers traveled northward through France into Belgium, Luxembourg, and Holland, lending vital support along the way to American infantry divisions battling the German army. In March 1945, the battalion received orders to return to southern France to help lead a massive Allied drive into Germany. The tankers continued fighting across Germany and into Austria, where they met up with the Russian army in May.

The war was coming to a close, and the men of the 761st Tank Battalion had played an important role in helping to bring about Germany's surrender. Unfortunately, however, Americans at home, especially white Americans, knew little or nothing about this accomplished unit; even some American forces fighting in Europe were unaware of the battalion's existence.

The 761st Tank Battalion was one of several African-American combat units to serve with distinction in World War II. Many of its members left the war as highly decorated soldiers, only to come back to a land of racism and segregation. It took thirty-three years for the American government to recognize their bravery and acknowledge the battalion's spectacular fighting record. In 1978, the Carter administration belatedly awarded the 761st Tank Battalion one of the highest military honors bestowed on a combat unit—the Presidential Unit Citation. The surviving men of the 761st finally felt satisfied; their story would not be forgotten.

Chapter 2
Wrath and Indignation

History has a way of repeating itself, especially in the case of African-American soldiers. From the Revolutionary War to the Persian Gulf War, African Americans have joined in every effort to preserve America's independence and to fight for world democracy. They have done so out of love for their country and with the hope that each successive battle will bring new freedoms and rewards to all African Americans. This was true during the beginning days of World War II, as well.

September 1, 1939, signaled the start of World War II in Europe when Hitler's German army invaded Poland. The United States, however, tried to remain neutral. With memories of World War I still fresh in the nation's mind, it did not want to get involved in another war across the Atlantic. Nor did America want to entangle itself in the Pacific, where Japan was attacking its Asian neighbors.

At the time, the United States' peacetime army

was considerably smaller than it had been at the end of World War I, with African Americans serving in only a limited capacity. By the end of 1939, there were just five black officers in the segregated army: three were chaplains, and the other two were Colonel Benjamin O. Davis and his son Lieutenant Benjamin O. Davis, Jr. Davis Sr. was the highest-ranking African-American soldier and would soon become the first black general in the United States Army. His son too would have his share of "firsts," commanding the army's first squadron of black aviators and becoming the air force's first black general.

In an effort to make some positive changes in the military, a group of African Americans formed the Committee on Participation of Negroes in the National Defense Program. It was the committee's hope that more African Americans would have the opportunity to serve not only as enlisted personnel but also as officers in the armed forces should the United States enter the war. The group also wanted to see more blacks assigned to combat positions.

As Germany's war in Europe continued into 1940, the committee as well as black veterans of World War I and the black press began to urge President Franklin D. Roosevelt to make sure the War Department would not discriminate against African Americans in any war effort. When the

Selective Training and Service Act, which called for 800,000 young men to be drafted into the armed forces, was approved in September of that year, it contained the clause: "there shall be no discrimination against any person on account of race or color."

This antidiscrimination clause of the Selective Service Act gave African-American leaders hope. But when three prominent African Americans—Walter White, secretary of the National Association for the Advancement of Colored People (NAACP); T. Arnold Hill, director of the National Urban League's Department of Industrial Relations; and A. Philip Randolph, president of the Brotherhood of Sleeping Car Porters (a black railroad labor union he organized)—met with President Roosevelt and his advisers, they were disappointed and angered to learn that the clause did not specifically mean an end to segregation in the military.

However, 1940 was an election year, and if Roosevelt hoped to win the black vote, he and his cabinet would have to make some concessions. Black leaders presented several demands, three of which were the abolition of segregation in the armed forces, the promotion of Colonel Benjamin O. Davis, Sr., to the rank of brigadier general, and the appointment of Judge William H. Hastie, dean of Howard University Law School, as assistant secretary in the War Department.

The White House yielded on most of the demands and agreed to organize more black combat units as well as to begin training black aviators, but it refused to end military segregation. African-American leaders thought, however, that Judge Hastie's newly created post as civilian aide to Secretary of War Henry Stimson would help bring about integration in the military. Yet Hastie had a rough road ahead of him, for Stimson believed, "Leadership is not imbedded in the negro race."

A. Philip Randolph was not satisfied with these few gains he and the other African-American leaders had made. He next turned his attention to bringing about changes in the hiring practices of defense-related industries.

The National Defense Training Act of 1940, designed to help train workers for war-related production jobs, contained an antidiscrimination clause, yet African Americans accounted for less than 3 percent of the men and women being trained for such jobs. To Randolph, these figures were evidence that African Americans needed to unite to protest such treatment. He conceived a plan to have thousands of blacks—and only blacks—march down the streets of Washington, D.C., on July 1, 1941. The march would show their disapproval of the government's lax enforcement of antidiscrimination policies and focus attention on their demands for equal rights in employment.

Five days before the march, President Roosevelt responded by issuing Executive Order 8802, which stated, "there shall be no discrimination in the employment of workers in defense industries or government because of race, creed, color, or national origin." The president also established a committee on fair employment practices to investigate complaints of discrimination. Although the order failed to address the issue of segregation in the armed forces, Randolph was pleased that the threat of a march had forced the Roosevelt administration into action. The march was canceled.

Randolph later explained, "When the defense program began and billions of the taxpayers' money were appropriated for guns, ships, tanks, and bombs, Negroes presented themselves for work only to be given the cold shoulder . . . . Not until their wrath and indignation took form . . . did things begin to move in the form of defense jobs for Negroes."

As more African Americans found work in defense-related industries, other young black men were anxious to have a chance to serve their country more actively in the armed forces. Many believed that they would experience less prejudice than their counterparts had in previous wars because of the antidiscrimination clause in the Selective Service Act. It wasn't until they arrived at their first military posts that the reality of Jim Crowism began to sink in for many of them. The phrase "Jim Crow" refers to segregation laws that were established to separate blacks from whites in communities across the United States, especially in the South, during the end of the nineteenth century and the early part of the twentieth century.

"To be a black soldier in the South in those days," recalled Johnnie Stevens, a veteran sergeant of the 761st Tank Battalion, "was one of the worst things that could happen to you." Yet Stevens, who grew up in Georgia and was raised under Jim Crow laws, had learned to live with segregation. "It really didn't bother me too much," he remembered, "but to the fellows who weren't used to it, it was tough." Another Southern veteran of the 761st, Preston McNeil, agreed: "My [Northern] comrades did not understand about segregation. . . . . They couldn't understand the sign that says, 'Colored,' 'White.'" McNeil cautioned the men to abide by the law when they were in the South; if they didn't, they'd only be asking for trouble.

Jim Crow laws even extended to the nation's blood banks. The American Red Cross insisted that blood from black and white donors remain segregated. This meant that blood taken from a

Negro donor could only be given to a wounded Negro soldier, and "white blood" could only be used for a white soldier. Yet scientists knew at the time that different blood groups were based on specific blood types, not on race.

Dr. Charles R. Drew, an African American in charge of surgery at Howard University's School of Medicine, tried to challenge the Red Cross's methods, saying that "the whole question of race of donors is a social one." He explained, "When a blood transfusion is given, the donor's blood must be compatible with that of the recipient, that is, Group or Type A blood from an individual of any race would be suitable for transfusion into the veins of an individual of any race providing it is blood of the same group." However, the American Red Cross refused to change its racist policy.

One unexpected ally that African-American soldiers had in their fight against racism was the nation's first lady, Eleanor Roosevelt. She was an ardent supporter of equal rights, and black leaders befriended her, knowing that her opinions could directly influence her husband. Mary McLeod Bethune, founder of the National Council of Negro Women and director of the Division of Negro Affairs of the National Youth Administration, used her privileged relationship with the first lady to voice the collective concerns of the nation's black leaders. One such issue was the lack of black advisers in the War Department; shortly afterward, President Roosevelt appointed William Hastie civilian aide to Secretary of War Stimson.

As Bethune appealed to Mrs. Roosevelt to convince the president to "come to the aid of blacks," Eleanor herself not only spoke to her husband but also attempted to influence her husband's advisers, often writing them personal letters to explain her views. Eleanor was especially sympathetic to the plight of black servicemen. Early in the war, she announced, "The nation cannot expect colored people to feel that the United States is worth defending if the Negro continues to be treated as he is now."

A. Philip Randolph and Mrs. Eleanor Roosevelt

Chapter 3
Training for War

The early morning hours of December 7, 1941, signaled America's entry into World War II when Japanese bombers attacked the naval base at Pearl Harbor, Hawaii. Aboard the battleship *West Virginia*, in the confusion of sirens, falling bombs, fire, and thick smoke, an African-American navy messman named Dorie Miller jumped into action. He moved his wounded captain out of the range of enemy fire and then took a place behind a machine gun at one of the ship's battle stations. Although he had never been trained on the gun, Miller attempted to shoot down Japanese fighter planes. For his courage in the face of danger, the navy awarded him the Navy Cross, making Dorie Miller one of the first heroes of the war.

Citizens throughout the country were outraged at Japan's attack. The next day, President Roosevelt went before Congress to ask that a state of war be declared. He referred to December 7, 1941, as "a date which will live in infamy." The Senate voted unanimously for war; the House had one dissent. Three days later, Germany and Italy declared war on the United States, and Congress reciprocated and formally declared war on those two countries as well.

By January 1942, the first American soldiers were sent overseas. These first soldiers, however, were white; African-American soldiers were not sent until May, and most of them were used as laborers. It would be another three years before the men of the 761st Tank Battalion would be called into action.

Before Japan's attack on Pearl Harbor, army officials had been debating whether or not African-American soldiers should be trained in armored warfare. The chief of the Army Ground Forces, Lieutenant General Leslie J. McNair, believed that black tankers would have a role to play if America entered the war. He was in favor of sending black soldiers to Fort Knox, Kentucky, for armored training, but his colleagues were skeptical of the idea. McNair eventually convinced the army to start an experimental tank training program at Fort Knox for African-American soldiers, and the first group of soldiers arrived there in March 1941. The black tank group was not designated as a separate battalion until June when it received word that it would be known as the 758th Tank Battalion.

After several months of tank training, the 758th moved to Camp Claiborne, Louisiana. New recruits trained at Fort Knox before joining the battalion in Louisiana. By April 1942, more and more black tankers began arriving at Camp Claiborne, and another African-American tank outfit was formed—the 761st Tank Battalion. It was the second of three all-black tank outfits created under the War Department's experimental project; the 784th Tank Battalion was the last unit to be organized. Recruits from Fort Knox joined the 761st, as well as some of the tankers who were attached to the 758th Tank Battalion. When the 761st was activated, there were 27 officers and 313 enlisted men.

Two men who went through officers' training at Fort Knox were David Williams and Charles Gates. Williams, who was white, had been drafted into a white tank unit as a private in January 1941, and after Pearl Harbor, he was sent to officers' school. Gates had been inducted into the service in April 1941 and had served with the all-black 10th Cavalry before being sent to Fort Knox.

As a native of Pennsylvania, David Williams had heard about segregation but had never seen it firsthand until he got to Louisiana. "I remember

E. G. McConnell, age sixteen, at Fort Knox

getting on the bus," he recalled, "and seeing all the Negroes sitting and standing behind a white line near the back of the bus. I wondered about that, then as I looked out and saw the little black towns along the way, suddenly . . . segregation hit me over the head."

E. G. McConnell, one of the youngest soldiers in the battalion, never forgot his first trip to the Deep South. He had been raised in a mixed ethnic neighborhood outside New York City, and as a young black man, he had never really experienced segregation until he joined the army. "As the train was chugging through the hills in Kentucky," he recalled, "orders came down for us to pull our

23

shades down. It was just us; we were in the first couple of cars because that's where blacks always rode—behind the locomotive, where you got all the soot, smoke, and noise. My curiosity got the the best of me. Why did we have to pull down the shades? Well, I went in between the two cars to look out, and I saw all these people, . . . some waving at the train with their guns. I later found out it was for our own security because there had been incidents where they fired at cars with black troops."

When McConnell eventually arrived at Camp Claiborne, he, like the rest of the men in the battalion, discovered that the black section of the base was not only located near the sewage treatment plant but "was filthy, smelly, and . . . infested with roaches." "Camp Claiborne was the end of the world," Johnnie Stevens remembered. "It was hot, swampy, full of mosquitoes, snakes, and anything else you can name." Sergeant Eddie Donald recalled that the black soldiers were "quartered . . . [in] the most undesirable area of the whole camp. White soldiers were at the other end of the camp, on good ground with the highway nearby and bus facilities to take them to town. We were strictly and completely segregated." The white officers assigned to the battalion, however, stayed with their men in the black section.

In the beginning, all of the officers of the 761st Tank Battalion were white, but as David Williams soon learned, many of his white comrades wanted nothing to do with a black tank unit. They were often in a hurry to leave the 761st and be reassigned to a white outfit. Williams stayed, though, eventually earning the reputation, as one soldier put it, as "the blackest white man you would ever want to know."

Before 1942 ended, the 761st Tank Battalion received its first group of black officers, and Charles Gates was among them. He remembered how difficult training became in the cold, damp Louisiana winter: "Immediately, we'd get in the field and the [fellows] would jump out of the tanks and start building fires. I called all my platoon in and told them, 'Now, gentlemen, . . . the first thing for you to do is concentrate on learning how best to use these things. My first order of the day is put out those . . . fires and get in those tanks . . . . When you see me working, that means you work.'" Gates soon won his men's respect, and he became affectionately known as "Pop" Gates.

One of the battalion's black officers was future baseball Hall of Famer Jackie Robinson, who stayed with the battalion until it went overseas. Before being drafted into the army, Robinson had been an all-star athlete at the University of California at Los Angeles. Part of his assignment with the 761st was as morale officer, and one way he boosted the men's spirits was by organizing baseball games. After leaving the army, Robinson went on to break major league baseball's color barrier when he joined the Brooklyn Dodgers in 1947.

Although the tanks the men initially trained in were light tanks, the ones they eventually drove into battle were medium tanks called General Shermans. There was room for five soldiers in a Sherman tank, and each man had a specific job to do. Three men sat in the top portion of the tank, called the turret, and two men sat in the bottom, toward the front. Looking forward from inside the tank, the two men seated at the top right were the tank commander and, in front of him, the gunner. To the gunner's left was the cannoneer. The driver sat in front of the cannoneer in the bottom part of the tank, and to the driver's right was the bow gunner/assistant driver.

The tank commander called the firing order and manned a 50–caliber machine gun. The gunner was in charge of the main gun mounted on the tank, while the cannoneer had the job of loading the shells into the main gun. The bow gunner/assistant driver operated a smaller machine gun and helped the driver maneuver the tank. E. G. McConnell recalled a typical firing order: "*Gunner,* addressing the gunner; *Tank*, telling him the type of target; *AP*, telling the cannoneer the type of ammunition to load (AP means armor-piercing); *Traverse Right*, telling the gunner where to aim the big gun; *Steady On*, giving the driver directions; *Range*, tank commander calls out an estimate of how close they are to the target; then *Fire!*"

The men in the tank heard these orders through a radio intercom that the tank commmander used. With the flip of a switch they could also listen to what was going on elsewhere on the field. In addition, each tanker wore a small microphone positioned close to his throat that allowed him to talk to his comrades inside the tank.

The driver, one of five soldiers assigned to a tank

Training progressed, and in April 1943, the 761st left Camp Claiborne to participate in army maneuvers with a number of different infantry divisions. These maneuvers simulated actual combat, helping the participants sharpen their skills and get a taste of what true combat could be like. In war, a tank battalion like the 761st would be assigned to an infantry division—a unit twice its size composed of foot soldiers.

The military organizes its forces by an "order of battle," beginning with the smallest fighting unit and building from there. Larger units are always composed of a certain number of smaller ones. The smallest unit is a squad, and a number of squads make a platoon. In the 761st Tank Battalion, for example, four to five platoons made a company, and there were six companies in the battalion. From a battalion, the battle order grows to a regiment, a division, a corps, and then to an army.

Lieutenant General Leslie McNair, who had originally proposed the formation of an African-American tank outfit, was on hand to watch the 761st on its first maneuvers. McNair told the tankers how pleased he was with their performance. His words strengthened the men's confidence in their abilities, and the battalion returned to Camp Claiborne in high spirits in June 1943.

Soldiers cleaning a machine gun during Third Army maneuvers

Chapter 4

Second-Class Treatment

Little could dampen the battalion's newfound enthusiasm, except perhaps a trip to the town outside Camp Claiborne, which was Alexandria, Louisiana. "To go into town," E. G. McConnell recalled, "we'd line up down at the bus station on camp. There was a black line and a white line. A bus would pull in, and they would allow [only] 10 or 12 blacks on the bus . . . all the way to the rear. Then the bus was filled to capacity with white troops." The remaining black soldiers would be left waiting, sometimes for hours, for the ride into town. Once they arrived in Alexandria, they had to stay on the black side of town. As Eddie Donald remembered, "We learned, with some difficulty, to accept this."

What was unacceptable to Donald and the rest of the black soldiers stationed at Camp Claiborne was the treatment German prisoners were given. These prisoners had been brought over to the

United States and placed at various holding camps throughout the country. At Claiborne, Donald recalled, "I noticed that a number of German prisoners were in the camp in a special area, not swampland. They were given freedom of movement and had access to facilities denied [to] black American soldiers. They were given passes to town when black soldiers were confined to the area . . . . This was one of the most repugnant things . . . that happened to Negro servicemen." McConnell agreed: "Here we were, first-class Americans, never been in prison, never been in war. Weren't prisoners of war or anything like that. And they would smirk at us, because they knew that they could go to any PX [post exchange store] on the post and purchase whatever they wanted."

Frustrated by what he had seen of the army's second-class treatment of African-American soldiers and the War Department's refusal to listen to any of his ideas, William Hastie resigned from his position as civilian aide to the secretary of war in 1943. He was especially upset about discrimination in the army's air forces. When Hastie had accepted his job as civilian aide, he understood that he would have a say in government policies relating to African Americans. However, after he disapproved a plan for a segregated training program for Negro pilots, the army stopped including Hastie in the decision-making process. Angry, Hastie called the army's Negro pilot training program "an 'experiment' designed to determine whether [a Negro] can do this or that in the field of aviation . . . [based on] unscientific notions that race somehow controls a man's capacity and attitudes."

In an effort to appease the black community after Hastie's resignation, the War Department finally decided to send the all-black 99th Pursuit Squadron, headed by Benjamin O. Davis, Jr., into combat. The "Lonely Eagles," as the members of this segregated group of black pilots were known, distinguished themselves fighting in the Mediterranean. However, by the end of 1943, they were still the only African-American unit to see combat. America had been at war for nearly two years.

Chicago attorney Truman K. Gibson, Jr., replaced William Hastie as the civilian aide to the secretary of war, and like Hastie, Gibson continued to push the Pentagon to utilize more African-American soldiers in the war effort. Many black soldiers were becoming disillusioned, wondering if they would ever get the chance to fight. Their mounting frustration often led to racial clashes with white soldiers.

Throughout 1943, the United States experienced a wave of racial violence in its cities and on its military bases. In Detroit, Michigan, a series of small fights between blacks and whites escalated into a huge riot that lasted for several days. By the time the situation was brought under control, 34 people had been killed, 25 of them black; 600 people had been injured; and more than 1,800 citizens were arrested. In New York City, a false rumor that an African-American soldier had been killed in front of his mother by a white policeman enraged thousands of black citizens, who took to the streets in protest. Their anger led to widespread looting.

Camp Claiborne was not immune to racial

Two soldiers assist a man during racial disturbances in New York City

violence. The 761st Tank Battalion was but one small unit of African-American soldiers at Claiborne. Out of the 48,000 soldiers stationed there, close to 8,500 were black. In the summer of 1943, according to one historian, "there was a chain of disturbances . . . including mass raids on post exchanges; . . . attempts by soldiers to overturn buses; and a near riot in a service club when an angry crowd [protested] the mistreatment of a black enlisted man by a white officer."

In mid-September, the men of the 761st left the hardships of Camp Claiborne behind and moved to Camp Hood, Texas, with their new commander Major Paul L. Bates. By late October, the unit was reorganized from a light tank battalion to a medium tank battalion, which meant it would be using the heavier Sherman tanks in all the companies except the newly formed Dog, or D, Company—this company would be composed solely of light tanks. This brought the number of companies in the 761st Tank Battalion up to six: Able (or A), Baker (B), Charlie (C), Dog (D), Service, and Headquarters. The Companies A, B, C, and D were combat units, while Service Company was responsible for keeping the battalion supplied with equipment, ammunition, food, and other necessities. Headquarters Company maintained the battalion's personnel files, but it also provided support with its vehicle maintenance platoon, assault gun platoon, mortar platoon, and reconnaissance platoon.

Sergeant Johnnie Stevens of A Company remembered Camp Hood as "hot, dusty, and dry. And outside the base, the conditions for blacks were the same as at Claiborne." To Private E. G. McConnell of Headquarters Company, discrimination on base was intolerable: "I was thoroughly disgusted with the U.S. Army and how they were treating us . . . . I was a good soldier, but the South and segregation made me want to get out of the army."

McConnell's enthusiasm for the military life had changed drastically. Only sixteen years old when he volunteered in May 1942, McConnell lied about his age to get into the service because as he remembered, "I knew I had a lot to help out with . . . . Everyone was patriotic at the time. We all felt a responsibility to participate in this [war]." By the time the 761st Tank Battalion reached Camp Hood, though, McConnell had tried several times to get himself thrown out of the army. His ploys failed to work. Instead of getting discharged, he was either denied passes to town or given extra duties.

The rest of the battalion busied itself refining its warfare tactics. According to Charles Gates, who

"All the reports coming up to Washington about you have been of a superior nature, and we are expecting great things of your battalion in combat."

was a first lieutenant in charge of Headquarters' assault gun platoon at the time, "We trained against the men in the antitank divisions, and we were very fortunate to outsmart them because we were so tiny. But we established quite a reputation." At a troop inspection with all the units of the entire camp lined up in formation, Lieutenant General Ben Lear, former commanding general of the Army Ground Force Reinforcement System, recognized the 761st's achievements: "All the reports coming up to Washington about you have been of a superior nature, and we are expecting great things of your battalion in combat."

Of course, many of the men in the 761st still didn't believe the unit would ever see combat. The battalion had been training for three years now, and when the Allied forces invaded German-occupied France on June 6, 1944, known as D-Day, the men's hopes of being sent overseas sank even further. Yet three days later, the battalion was caught by surprise when it was put on alert for overseas duty. Orders from the War Department specified that an advance party would leave on July 20 for Camp Kilmer, New Jersey, and the rest of the battalion would follow on August 10, 1944, and proceed to Camp Shanks, New York.

Two and a half weeks after arriving at Camp Shanks, the battalion sailed for England on the

British ship H.M.S. *Esperance Bay*. As the ship pulled out of New York Harbor, the men were in high spirits, even Private E. G. McConnell. "They really needed me," McConnell recalled, "because I was one of two who had received training on this top secret gyrostabilizer in the tank. I was a very necessary part of this team." McConnell was with the vehicle maintenance platoon of Headquarters Company and had taken advanced courses in tank maintenance at Fort Knox.

"On the trip going over," explained Johnnie Stevens, "we were jam-packed and sick most of the time." McConnell especially remembered the sleeping conditions on board: "In the bowels of the boat, there were swinging hammocks five high. You had to use a pole with pegs to get to the top hammock."

As the *Esperance Bay* steamed across the Atlantic, other African-American units were beginning to see action, in addition to the "Lonely Eagles" of the 99th Pursuit Squadron. The men of the 93rd Infantry Divison had been deployed to the Pacific earlier in 1944 to join the war against Japan, while the 92nd Infantry Division did its part combating enemy forces in Italy. The soldiers of the 761st Tank Battalion were more than ready to join the other African-American soldiers already playing an active role in the war.

Chapter 5

"Don't Let Me Down!"

The 761st Tank Battalion landed in England on September 8, 1944, and traveled to the small town of Wimborne in southern England to await equipment and further orders. Unlike other black troops sent to England, the men of the 761st experienced few problems with racism, "except," as E. G. McConnell remembered, "with owners of pubs who were catering to discrimination." Many of the race problems in England were between white and black American soldiers, and did not involve the British people themselves.

Four weeks after their arrival, the men of the 761st received word that they would be fighting in General George S. Patton's Third Army. They were to proceed across the English Channel to France. The battalion was at full strength with 36 officers and 676 enlisted men.

"We landed at Omaha Beach," recalled Johnnie Stevens, " . . . and from what we saw, we knew we were going into combat." McConnell never forgot that day: "As we approached the coast, there were sunken ships and debris everywhere. I never saw so much devastation in my life. How could anyone lose this much and still wage a major war?"

As the 761st traveled through France in their brand new Sherman tanks, French citizens came out of their homes with gifts of flowers and champagne to welcome the black American tankers. The men were flattered, and their morale stayed high.

After traveling 400 miles without encountering any enemy resistance, the battalion stopped at the French town of Saint-Nicholas-de-Port on October 28. There the men made last-minute equipment checks and met the division they would be

A gunner stands ready in France, 1944

supporting—the 26th Infantry. They were close enough to the front line to hear the sounds of battle a few miles away. The soldiers had no illusions about war, especially after learning that the 26th Infantry had recently lost close to 400 men in battle in one afternoon.

Five days later, on November 2, 1944, General Patton visited the 761st Tank Battalion and left a lasting impression on all its members. Standing on a vehicle called a half-track that had wheels in the front and tank tracks in the back, Patton addressed his new tank outfit: "Men, you're the first Negro tankers to ever fight in the American Army. I would never have asked for you if you weren't good. I have nothing but the best in my Army. I don't care what color you are, so long as you go up there and kill those [Germans]. Everyone has their eyes on you and is expecting great things from you. Most of all, your race is looking forward to you. Don't let them down, and . . . don't let me down!"

After his speech, the men were given the signal to "mount up," and Patton climbed down from the half-track and went over to inspect the tanks. "He climbed up on top of my tank on the commander's side," recalled E. G. McConnell. "I was on the cannoneer's side, and he climbed down and looked me straight in the eye. He said, 'Boy,

I want you to use these . . . guns and shoot up every . . . thing you see—churches, graveyards, houses, . . . haystacks. You hear me. . . ?'" The young private was awestruck. He could only respond, "Yes, General."

On November 7, the battalion received a visit from an African-American army war correspondent named Trezzvant Anderson, who would spend the next several months detailing the accomplishments of the 761st Tank Battalion in regular dispatches that he would send back to the United States. However, only black newspapers printed the articles. The rest of the American press ignored them, which only helped to foster more ignorance about the role African-American soldiers played during World War II. Anderson became the battalion's self-appointed historian, and at the end of the war, he wrote a book, entitled *Come Out Fighting*, about the deeds of these brave tankers.

The next day the battalion entered battle for the first time. Johnnie Stevens remembered that day: "I had never been in combat before, and there was something exciting about going in. You know you've trained . . . you can do the job, but you're just wondering what it's going to be like."

"The tension was great," recalled David Williams, who commanded A Company. "We had a meeting with the sergeants, and my driver got black greasepaint and put it on my face. He said, 'We hear they shoot officers, and you stick out among us.' The men just laughed and one of them said, 'Hey, you look good as a nigger.' After that, somehow I knew things were going to be all right."

Captain John D. Long, commander of B Company, confided, "I expected to get killed, but whatever happened I was determined to die an officer and a gentleman." Long, who started his army career as a cook at Fort Knox, had come a long way. After graduating from officers' training school, he became one of the first black lieutenants in the tank corps. Like Long, another cook had aspirations of fighting for his country. His name was Walter Lewis, and although some of the sergeants of A Company thought he was a sissy, his commander, Captain Williams, knew that he was a good gunner and found a place for him in one of the company's tanks.

The first tank to move into battle that day was one of A Company's tanks, commanded by Staff Sergeant Ruben Rivers, who would earn the reputation of "leading the way." The 761st Tank Battalion and the 26th Infantry had been told that their objective was to cut off all German supply and escape routes to and from the northern city of Metz, France. For the 761st, this meant securing more than two dozen towns from Athainville,

France, to the German border fifty miles away.

Under cloudy skies and drizzling rain, the men went into battle against one of Germany's elite tank divisions. The tankers and infantrymen met with strong resistance from the Germans, but as the day wore on, the Americans gained the edge, pushing the Germans back and capturing three towns in the process. Ruben Rivers showed his fearlessness that day when he dismounted his tank under heavy enemy fire to remove a roadblock. His willingness to face danger in order to complete his mission earned Ruben Rivers a Silver Star.

The 761st Tank Battalion's first day in battle was not without losses. C Company took the hardest pounding, losing an entire tank crew and three

A tank on the road in France, 1944

43

of its tanks. One of the unit's medics was killed that day, and the battalion's commander was seriously wounded. But, as Trezzvant Anderson wrote, "the initial fear was gone, and the men had assumed the feeling of seasoned vets."

At 9:00 AM the next day the 761st coordinated an attack on its next objective: the town of Morville-les-Vic. After taking the town of Chateau-Salins, A Company continued eastward, advancing on the left side of Morville. C Company approached from the northwest, while B Company advanced in between the other two companies. D Company provided cover from the northeast. The 26th Infantry followed behind the tanks of B Company.

Captain Long, commander of B Company, remembered how fierce the fighting was that day: "The town . . . was supposed to be a snap, but it was an inferno. A German officer we captured in the town said the heroism of one of our tank crews in battle was only equaled by that of a Russian tank crew under similar circumstances. He was referring to a tank of B Company . . . which had been knocked out by a bazooka. Two wounded men of the tank crew were pulled to safety under their useless vehicle by their comrades who then seized automatic weapons, knocked out the bazooka that had disabled them, and put at least six German antitank gunners out of action."

C Company got caught in an antitank trap ditch that the Germans had constructed. The enemy had placed mines in front of the ditch and had built pillboxes—camouflaged, concrete structures containing antitank guns—twenty-five yards behind the ditch. The Germans knocked out seven tanks and killed ten men; the number would have been higher had it not been for the heroic efforts of First Sergeant Samuel Turley and Second Lieutenant Kenneth Coleman. These two men lost their lives helping direct their men to safety. They were both posthumously awarded Silver Stars for their "inspiring courage and strong devotion to duty."

Sergeant Eddie Donald of B Company recalled the Battle of Morville as a suicide mission: "We were told by our company commander that they had a little town over the hill they wanted us to take and we were going to spearhead . . . the division. This was the first time I had heard the word *spearhead* and I really did not know what it meant until the following morning. We were to go in and soften up the enemy; we really weren't expected to come out of it. We were supposed to soften up things so the troops behind us . . . could capture the town without too much difficulty."

"It was to be our first mission, also our last one," said Sergeant Horace Jones of Service Company. "How we got through that I don't know."

From Morville, the tankers continued heading northeast toward the German border. The weather began turning colder, but the men of the 761st were growing tougher day by day. Those first days of battle helped the men determine which methods worked best in locating and destroying enemy targets. Private McConnell, who by Morville had taken a position as a cannoneer with C Company, described one such method: "Instead of shooting the big gun at a target, we would fire the machine gun. Every fifth round was a tracer . . . that lit up in flight. [We'd] watch the tracers to get onto the target; the four rounds in between were just regular [bullets]. Once the stream was right on target . . . Boom! You'd hit the big gun. When the machine gun was on target so was the big gun."

The next big town after Morville was Guebling, France, where Johnnie Stevens' platoon had orders to support the infantry in taking a hill called Hill 309. He vividly recalled that day: "Usually the infantry is behind you because your job is to blast the bushes, the hills, knock out positions. Well, there wasn't supposed to be anything on that hill, but [the enemy] had set [a] trap . . . . They put anti-tank guns off to the side . . . and caught us in a crossfire. I got hit." After Stevens ejected from his tank, a white infantry sergeant helped roll him into a nearby ditch. The sergeant was then killed.

A tank from Company A, 761st Tank Battalion, U.S. Third Army, moves to a forward position in the combat zone in France, 1944

47

Stevens never knew who the infantry sergeant was who saved his life, but he's never forgotten that man's heroic deed.

Although African-American soldiers suffered from racism at home and in areas away from the fighting, the situation at the front lines was different. "During combat [segregation] did not exist," explained Ivan Harrison, a first lieutenant with Headquarters Company. "We fought side by side with the [white infantry divisions]," added Eddie Donald, "and we slept together and ate together."

On November 18, the 761st took the town of Guebling with Ruben Rivers leading the way. That evening his tank was disabled after hitting a land mine. Rivers, however, just climbed aboard another tank and continued to fight. The next morning as his new tank approached Guebling under heavy enemy fire, it also was hit, and Rivers was killed. The battalion lost a true hero that day.

Walter Lewis also displayed remarkable heroism in Guebling. After his tank was hit, he bailed out and began following the rest of his tank crew to safety. But when he realized that one of the crew hadn't made it out, he ran back to the tank under heavy fire and pulled the cannoneer out. Such calmness and courage under fire made it hard to believe that the men of the 761st Tank Battalion had been in combat for only ten days.

Chapter 6

The Battle of the Bulge

On November 25, the 761st Tank Battalion encountered the enemy near the town of Honskirch, where the fierce exchange of firepower reminded many of the men of the Battle of Morville. Although they had been steadily driving the Germans back, the men of the 761st recognized that Honskirch posed special problems. Not only was it a major crossroads, but the town sat at the base of a hill, allowing the Germans behind the town to have a clear view of all the incoming routes.

Captain Gates, now commanding C Company, was given orders by the infantry colonel to take the town of Honskirch. "His order was to go down the road straight," recalled Gates. "I tried to tell him that was not an effective way to use tanks."

Honskirch was the last of two objectives of the day. The company had already successfully taken one town, and as the tanks approached Honskirch, E. G. McConnell remembered, "We got an urgent call to withdraw." At the time, McConnell did not know the reason for the order, but he believed that the delay gave the Germans time to regroup.

From Gates' perspective, the mission was "in defiance of good tactics," and he decided to delay the attack for as long as possible. But after four hours, the infantry colonel gave Gates a direct order to move his tanks into the town, and so the eleven tanks proceeded down the road in a column.

"Then the very thing I told him would happen, happened," Gates later said. "We got on the road . . . the Germans threw a shell in front of the first tank and fired on the last tank to stop the platoon. In less than five minutes, five tanks were destroyed."

Gates and McConnell were among the wounded. One man died, and his death left Gates bitter about taking orders. He recalled, "I made up my mind that day: since I'm going to be on the front, I [couldn't care] less . . . what [a commanding officer's] rank is. I will tell my men whether they can perform the operation." His men were his responsiblity, and Gates would not jeopardize their safety a second time.

The wounded were evacuated and taken to nearby hospitals, but the rest of the 761st pressed on, battling the enemy in town after town. By early

December Companies A, B, and C had made it to the Maginot Line. The Maginot Line was a string of fortresses that France had built in the 1930s along its border with Germany. The line was thought to be impenetrable, but the Germans proved otherwise.

From there, the battalion split up, with A Company heading southeast and C Company traveling northeast. The German border was their goal. On December 14, after traveling through heavily booby-trapped areas, the 761st crossed into Germany, and according to Trezzvant Anderson, "it was the first time in history that Negro tankers had ever been on German soil!"

The men hardly had time to catch their breath before they were ordered to Belgium. The 87th Infantry Division had now replaced the tired men of the 26th Division, but for the black tankers there was no rest and there were no replacements. The men of the 761st did, however, have a chance to celebrate the holiday season.

David Williams recalled, "The guys got a little Christmas tree and decorated it with cotton on Christmas Eve. Then the next day we . . . had a traditional turkey dinner that Walter [Lewis] cooked. We were . . . nice [and] warm, had the fires going, and had a good night's sleep."

The calm didn't last long. The men were

woken up at two o'clock the next morning with orders to proceed to a place called Bastogne, Belgium. "At the time," explained Williams, "we didn't know the significance of it." The battalion arrived near the front lines in Belgium on December 31, 1944, New Year's Eve.

It was bitterly cold and snowing in this hilly, forested region known as the Ardennes, where the countries of Belgium, Luxembourg, and France meet. Since autumn, Allied troops had been successful in forcing the German army back toward its border, especially north and south of the Ardennes. With each Allied victory, Germany's dictator Adolf Hitler refused to admit defeat; he was confident that his troops would battle back.

After studying a map of the entire European battlefield, Hitler recognized a weakness in the Allied defense line in the Ardennes. Spotting this, he constructed a plan to catch his enemies off guard by secretly massing a huge German force in the region. His soldiers would then attack the Allies and push them back toward the west coast of Belgium.

On December 16, Hitler ordered his army to attack, and by December 22, the Germans had created a huge bulge in the Allied defense line that extended almost forty miles into Belgium. The attack had definitely surprised the Allied commanders, and it cost them dearly. Ground was lost, and many soldiers were killed. The Allies, however, were able to halt the Germans' advance near the town of Bastogne, and troop reinforcements were called in to help in the battle now known as the Battle of the Bulge.

When the 761st arrived in the area, its first job was to capture two towns fifteen miles west of Bastogne, which it did with the help of a regiment of the 87th Infantry Division. Its main objective, though, was to take the town of Tillet west of Bastogne. Many of the veterans of the 761st felt the battle for Tillet was one of the worst battles they ever fought. They were fighting the enemy as well as the weather.

Of Tillet, Trezzvant Anderson wrote, "Not a single man who went through the battle there will ever forget the memories of those rugged days, when the enemy withstood the most vicious armored attacks the 761st could fling at him. . . . Tillet was the beginning of the end."

The companies of the battalion coordinated their attack on the town, and as the men began testing the enemy, they realized they were facing one of the same German divisions they had fought in France. "It might sound odd," explained Eddie Donald, "but if you have a return engagement with a unit, you know it. You recognize their style of fighting."

Captain Williams and the men of A Company decided to start their offensive by feigning an attack on the hillside in Gerimont, overlooking Tillet. Williams did not want to commit his men to battle right away without knowing what the Germans had on the other side of the hill. He knew that if his men went down the hill, they would not be able to retreat; the snow-covered ground was just too slippery. By faking an attack, Williams hoped to draw the enemy to him.

The tanks of A Company moved out slowly from their hiding places, with the inexperienced infantrymen of the 87th Division following behind. Just as David Williams spotted the uniforms of German soldiers, the group was fired upon. The company fired back, knocking out one of the Germans' tank destroyers. After that, the enemy started coming after the group just as Williams had hoped. One problem, though, was that the young infantrymen failed to move away from the tanks after the firing started. Williams remembered, "They were all lying down on their faces frightened. [My staff sergeant] was kicking them and kicking them; he couldn't get these kids to move. Finally, they got up. Then, of course, it looked like a slaughterhouse with the artillery coming in and getting them."

The tanks and infantry retreated, and the next day, German soldiers came up the hill to engage the company in battle again. The Germans showered the group with artillery and mortar fire, and the men of A Company fought back, but Williams still wasn't ready to commit them completely to battle. He was waiting for reinforcements and more ammunition.

After several days of being provoked by the enemy, Captain Williams knew that a decision would have to be made. The Germans were getting restless, and Williams feared that by now they might have guessed his men were short on supplies; if so, he knew the enemy would probably launch a full attack the following morning. That's when he made up his mind to meet with his sergeants and have them decide A Company's fate.

When Walter Lewis spoke up and said they had to fight it out and not surrender, the rest of the men knew he was right. Surrendering would not guarantee their safety—they could get killed either way. The Germans did not have a reputation for being kind to their prisoners of war.

The next morning the Germans did not attack, but A Company did. The men crept down the hill through the early morning fog and snow. After they had traveled only about twenty yards or so, the fog lifted, and to their surprise, the Germans

After performing the
duties of battalion
adjutant and
personnel officer
simultaneously,
Warrant Officer
Clarence Godbold
earned a battlefield
promotion to Second
Lieutenant

were right in front of them. Both groups began to fire; this time they were committed to battle.

Elsewhere, the other companies of the 761st Tank Battalion were engaging the enemy in battle, with both sides losing men and tanks. Chilled to the bone, the weary men of the 761st kept fighting, and after five days, the Germans began to retreat. Tillet now belonged to the Americans. But as Eddie Donald explained, "You can find Tillet in many books on World War II, but you won't find one word about us."

In any case, the men of the 761st knew they had bested the German troops, and working with the 17th Airborne Division, they continued to chase the Germans out of Belgium.

"You can find Tillet in many books on World War II, but you won't find one word about us."

Chapter 7
The Beginning of the End

From Belgium, the 761st Tank Battalion moved into Holland in early February, where it was assigned to the 79th Infantry Division of the Ninth United States Army. It was here that the battalion welcomed back its original commander, Lieutenant Colonel Bates, and received 200 new recruits.

Charles Gates of C Company was put in charge of training the new men. Most of them were eager to serve with the 761st. Some of the recruits even took a reduction in rank to serve with the battalion. The 761st had gained quite a reputation among African-American servicemen; many considered it an honor to be part of the unit.

"As long as they could fire a machine gun," explained Johnnie Stevens, "we found a job for them. We could teach a guy to be a bow gunner or a cannoneer. The other technical stuff like using the panoramic sights and the gyrostabilizer would take months to learn. An experienced bow gunner could become a gunner because he had been trained for that too. We'd just move him up . . . and put the rookie in the bow gunner's position."

After several weeks of training, the battalion moved out of Holland and crossed the German border for the third time, capturing fleeing German soldiers along the way. As the 761st continued its drive into Germany, the battalion received orders to withdraw once again and head to southern France.

By the time the men of the 761st reached Saverne, France, in mid-March, they had been fighting continuously on the front line for five months. Now they were paired with the 103rd Infantry Division of the Seventh United States Army. There seemed to be no rest in sight for the African-American tankers.

The men learned that the entire Allied front was moving forward, from Holland to Switzerland, and the 761st Tank Battalion was given the difficult task of cracking Germany's Siegfried Line. So far, several other divisions, one of them an armored unit, had failed to make any progress in breaking through the line.

In 1938, Hitler decided to protect Germany's western border with a wall. He came up with a plan for a line of concrete and steel fortifications that would zigzag 400 miles northward along

Germany's borders with Switzerland, France, Luxembourg, Belgium, and Holland. Known as *Der Westwall*, the structure's first line of fortification consisted of rows and rows of large, concrete domes, called "dragon's teeth," meant specifically to stop tanks. Behind these concrete domes, concealed bunkers and pillboxes were built, linked to one another by concrete roads. The Germans completed the wall in August 1939. The Allies later called it "the Siegfried Line."

On March 21, 1945, the 761st Tank Battalion's commander, Lieutenant Colonel Paul Bates, was put in charge of a large combat unit that was nicknamed Task Force Rhine. The task force consisted of the entire 761st Tank Battalion, a battalion of infantrymen, a group of combat engineers, and a platoon of tank destroyers. This unit was given the job of breaking through the Siegfried Line and moving eastward to Germany's Rhine River.

The mountainous, wooded area that the task force had to travel through was full of hidden enemy antitank gun sites and mortar positions. Working together, the tankers and infantrymen disabled as many positions as they could, then the combat engineers came behind with explosives and demolished each disabled position.

The task force met stiff enemy resistance every

inch of the way, but it continued to press forward, gaining new ground each hour. One of the tank platoons developed a tactic that worked especially well in its attempts to capture towns. First, two tanks rushed into the town, while the other tanks provided cover. Then another two tanks would rush forward and so on. This platoon alone disabled forty-one enemy positions and captured 1,450 Germans, helping to smooth the way for the Allied troops following behind the task force.

The second day into its mission, Task Force Rhine split up into two units—one headed eastward, the other to the northeast. The eastward unit was forced to withdraw after encountering heavy enemy fire, but the northeast unit moved steadily forward, leaving only the dust and rubble of destroyed enemy positions behind it.

Task Force Rhine regrouped and headed northeastward to meet the 10th Armored Division in one of the small towns along the way to the Rhine. But as the men approached the town of Silz, they were greeted with a shower of enemy mortar and artillery fire; the 10th Armored Division was nowhere to be found. The task force could not turn back—they were in the middle of the Siegfried Line.

Fighting into the night, the task force took the small town and continued eastward, using the light from the burning town to guide its way. Sometime around midnight the tanks came upon a column of retreating enemy vehicles, many of them horse-drawn. The unit fired upon the column with devastating effect—men and horses were killed, vehicles were disabled, and artillery pieces were blown apart.

By four o'clock that morning, the group reached its final objective: the town of Klingenmunster, Germany. After half an hour of fighting, the task force entered and secured the town; they had passed through the Siegfried Line into the heart of Germany. The task force had accomplished its mission in just under seventy-two hours. The rear Allied divisions would now be able to cross safely into Germany.

Along the way to its objective, Task Force Rhine captured thousands of Germans, and the black tankers learned early on to wait until the surrendering enemy was almost abreast of them before giving any orders. Charles Gates remembered one anxious tanker who opened his hatch too soon: "The Germans saw him and said, '*Schwarzen Soldaten!*' Black soldiers! And they started running back to the woods. As hard a time as we had getting them out of those woods, we weren't going to let them back in. So I told [my men], 'Fire in a straight line over their heads, and when they see that the limbs of the trees ahead of them are coming down, they'll understand that if we want to, we can kill them.' They turned around and came back."

This was the 761st Tank Battalion's fifth time in Germany, and the men were determined that it would also be their last. On March 30, the battalion crossed the Rhine and met up with its new infantry division—the 71st—in Langenselbold, Germany. From there, the combined unit headed northeast toward the town of Fulda. The enemy was now in retreat, and although the unit encountered small pockets of resistance, overall the fighting became less intense. There were no more battles like Morville, Honskirch, and Tillet. The weather turned warmer, and life became easier for the weary tankers. Germans began surrendering to the 761st, and those German soldiers who could not bear the thought of surrendering to black soldiers fought to their deaths or committed suicide.

Town after town fell as the battalion moved southward toward Austria. On May 2, 1945, the 761st Tank Battalion reached Germany's border with Austria. Its orders were to cross into Austria and wait for Russian troops to join them at the Enns River. By May 5, a tank platoon of A Company had reached the town of Steyr, Austria, on the bank of the Enns. The next day, the battalion spotted the Russians on the opposite bank. Their

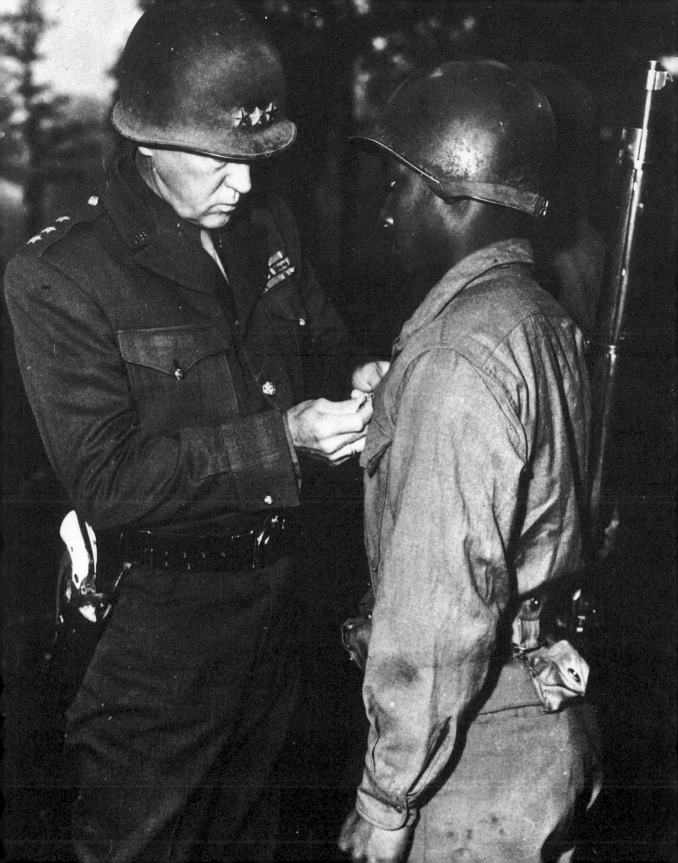

mission was complete. After traveling nearly 2,000 miles and fighting continuously for 183 days, the tired men of the 761st could finally rest.

"Not many hours later, as the tanks of the first Negro-composed armored unit . . . stood lined up beside a small bridge," Trezzvant Anderson wrote, "who should roll by in his . . . battlejeep, but . . . General George S. Patton, Jr.! There was a quiet satisfied look on [the] great warrior's face as he went on his way."

Many of the tankers not only earned Purple Hearts, but a number of the men also received Silver and Bronze Star medals for their courageous efforts. Yet one award that eluded these soldiers—and all black soldiers during World War II—was the Congressional Medal of Honor, America's highest decoration for heroism. The Second World War is the only war in which an African American <u>did not</u> win such an honor; yet the government deemed more than 400 white World War II veterans worthy of the medal.

If one man from the 761st Tank Battalion stands out in deserving such recognition, it is Staff Sergeant Ruben Rivers. Rivers, who always led his men fearlessly into battle, showed the depth of his devotion to his unit and to his country at Guebling, where he refused to leave the battlefield after being seriously wounded. He continued fighting, losing

General George S. Patton, Jr., pins a medal on the uniform of an African-American soldier his life, because he knew his men needed him—whatever the cost. His unselfishness made him a true hero to the men of the 761st.

Rivers's former company commander, David Williams, has been trying since 1945 to persuade the government to award a posthumous decoration. So far, his attempts have been unsuccessful, yet he and the surviving veterans of the 761st have not given up hope of securing a Medal of Honor for Rivers.

Anese Rivers Woodfork with a photograph of her brother, Ruben Rivers

Black Tank Veterans Fighting
Battle to Get Medal for Buddy

Highest Medal Sought
for GI Slain in 1944

Bart Bartholemew/The New York Times

Chapter 8

Indomitable Fighting Spirit

Two days after the 761st Tank Battalion met up with Russian troops in Austria, Germany formally surrendered. Three months later, on August 15, 1945, World War II officially came to a close when Japan surrendered. The men of the 761st knew that by the end of the year many of them would be going home. They, like all African-American soldiers, hoped their war efforts would be recognized and would help toward mending past racial conflicts.

Unfortunately, very few war correspondents bothered to visit or interview African-American combat troops during the war. The 761st Tank Battalion was no exception. Johnnie Stevens remembered how invisible the black tankers felt when, after capturing a town, press crews came in to interview the supporting infantry: "We'd complete a mission and up would roll the cameras, and they'd roll right past all of those big tanks . . .

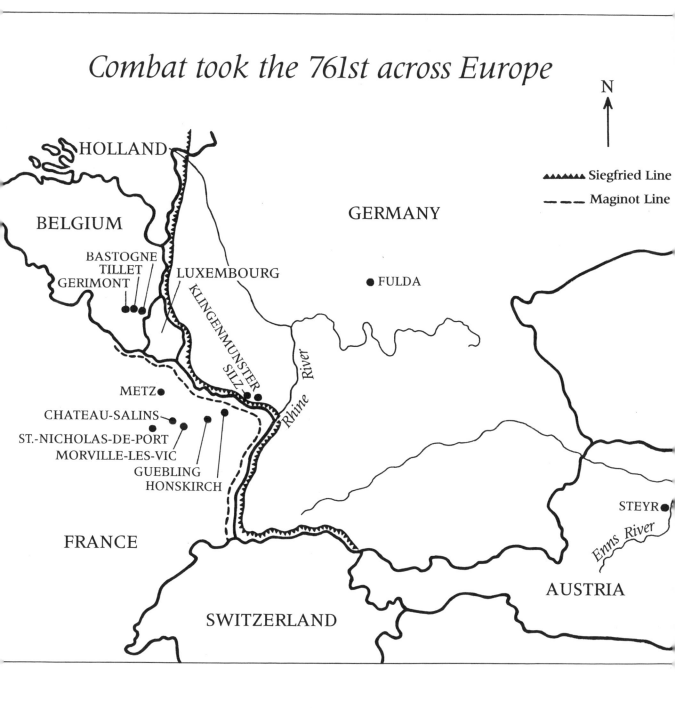

Combat took the 761st across Europe

roll right past us to where the white infantry were gathered and start taking pictures, asking what were their names and where were they from. Not once did they ever stop and take our pictures or get our names or ask where we were from."

The 761st Tank Battalion's record might have gone unrecognized by the press, but their efforts hardly escaped the notice of army commanders. After reaching Steyr, Austria, Lieutenant Colonel Paul Bates wanted to make sure his men knew how invaluable they were and how proud he was of their efforts. In a letter to all the officers and enlisted men of the 761st, Bates wrote: "You have fought gallantly in all extremes of climate and terrain . . . [that] have all caused you intense discomfort and greatly tried your ingenuity and ability. . . . You have met every type of equipment in the German Army. . . . All have hurt you. All have destroyed some of your equipment. But all are behind you, useless, the German soldier defeated, his politician silent, and you are victorious!"

Although the battalion lost only thirty-four men in combat, many more were wounded, and its casualty rate was 50 percent. The scars of war last a lifetime, and veterans of the 761st would carry reminders of the horrors they saw home with them; some would never forget the deadly sights and sounds of war.

"War is a strange thing," said John Long, the commander of B Company. "You are trained to do a job, even . . . the killing of men, but you do your job. It is an impersonal thing, at least it had better be or you are in for a lot of trouble."

More than a million African-American soldiers participated in World War II, half of whom were sent overseas to serve. Black women also did their part, becoming members of the Women's Army Auxiliary Corps (WAACs) and performing duties ranging from driving trucks to sorting mail.

"Being in an all-black outfit," recalled Eddie Donald, "I found my own experience with the . . . black soldier was that he performed no differently than white soldiers in terms of heroic deeds, in terms of his feelings towards typical war situations; moments of despair, moments of happiness. The Negro soldier felt the same emotions as did any other soldier."

During the entire war, the men of the 761st Tank Battalion had stayed together as a team. But when the war ended, most of the white officers serving with the battalion were sent back to the United States in September with white units, whether they liked it or not. The rest of the battalion left Europe several months later, coming home as a truly all-black unit with Captain Ivan Harrison of Headquarters Company commanding

the battalion.

For most African-American soldiers, homecoming was a mixed blessing. Although many African Americans had made some gains at home during the war, finding work in defense-related jobs and learning new skills, soldiers returning home after the war realized that little true progress had been made in the area of civil rights. This fact became brutally clear to one black sergeant named Isaac Woodard who had served in the South Pacific.

On his way home to North Carolina, the

Captain Ivan Harrison, left, with two other field officers of the 761st Tank Battalion uniformed Woodard was severely beaten by a South Carolina policeman after the driver of the bus on which Woodard was riding demanded that he be arrested for drunkenness. (Woodard was not drunk. The bus driver was angry that Woodard had taken too much time using the "colored only" restroom in an earlier town.) The ex-serviceman was denied any medical care following the beating and was thrown into jail for the night. The next morning he was fined $50 and released. When Woodard finally reached an army hospital, doctors declared him permanently blind; the beating he received had completely destroyed his sight.

News of Woodard's ordeal shocked the nation; even President Harry S Truman commented to Walter White, head of the NAACP, "I had no idea things were as terrible as that. We've got to do something." And he eventually did. In July 1948, Truman issued Executive Order 9981, permanently ending segregation in the armed forces. The order states, "It is hereby declared to be the policy of the President that there shall be equality of treatment and opportunity for all persons in the armed services without regard to race, color, religion or national origin."

Many of the men of the 761st left the army after the war for other jobs, but their strong bond of friendship could not be broken. In 1949, after the veterans had adjusted to their new lives, the 761st Tank Battalion had its first reunion, a yearly tradition that has continued to the present day. It was at one of these reunions that the men began discussing the fact that their outfit had been denied a Presidential Unit Citation (PUC)—the highest award given to a combat outfit. It was an award the men of the 761st felt they had earned.

It wasn't until eighteen years later, in 1977, that their dream of having someone review the 761st's combat record came true. Many of the veterans had been writing to the White House and the secretary of the army for years. They hoped that information they provided about the battalion would make someone curious enough to investigate why the 761st Tank Battalion had never been awarded a Presidential Unit Citation. Under the Carter administration, Secretary of the Army Clifford Alexander, an African American himself, assigned a team of researchers to the battalion's case.

In January 1978 after months of investigation, Charles Gates, who was the president of the 761st Tank Battalion and Allied Veterans Association at the time, received a personal phone call from Clifford Alexander. Alexander informed him that it appeared certain President Carter would be giving the battalion the Presidential Unit Citation. Four months later, on April 20, 1978, 200 veterans of

E. G. McConnell (left), with two other veterans, at one of the earliest reunions of the 761st

"For over thirty years you have lived with the knowledge that you did something out of the ordinary. The Army and the Nation share that knowledge today."

Lieutenant Colonel Charles A. ("Pop") Gates (Retired), at the left, accepts the certificate awarding the Presidential Unit Citation to the 761st Tank Battalion from Secretary of the Army, Clifford L. Alexander.

the 761st and their families gathered on the grounds of Fort Myer, Virginia, to receive their long overdue award. Speaking to the veterans, Secretary Alexander praised their wartime courage and accomplishments: "For over thirty years you have lived with the knowledge that you did something out of the ordinary. The Army and the Nation share that knowledge today." He then gave each surviving member of the tank battalion a signed letter from President Carter and a little blue pin to wear—a symbol to all servicemen that the wearer's combat unit was awarded the distinguished Presidential Unit Citation.

It is the letter that gives the veterans the most pride. In it, President Carter summarizes the battalion's history for all future generations to read and remember: "The 761st Tank Battalion distinguished itself by extraordinary gallantry, courage, professionalism and high *esprit de corps* displayed in the accomplishment of unusually difficult and hazardous operations in the European Theater of Operations from 31 October 1944 to 6 May 1945 . . . . Throughout this period of combat, the courageous and professional actions of the members of the 'Black Panther' battalion, coupled with their indomitable fighting spirit and devotion to duty, reflect great credit on the 761st Tank Battalion, the United States Army, and this Nation."

Chronology:

African Americans in the U.S. Armed Forces

1770	On March 5, Crispus Attucks, a former slave, is among the first to die in the "Boston Massacre."
1776-1781	7,000 African-American soldiers and sailors take part in the Revolutionary War.
1776	On January 16, the Continental Congress agrees to enlist free blacks.
1812-1815	Black soldiers and sailors fight against the British troops at such critical battles as Lake Erie and New Orleans.
1862-1865	186,000 African-American soldiers serve in black regiments during the Civil War; 38,000 black soldiers lose their lives in more than 400 battles.
1862	On July 17, the U.S. Congress approves the enlistment of black soldiers.
1865	On March 13, the Confederate States of America begins to accept black recruits.
1866-1890	Units of black soldiers, referred to as Buffalo Soldiers, are formed as part of the U.S. Army.
1872	On September 21, John H. Conyers becomes the first African American admitted to the U.S. Naval Academy.
1877	On June 15, Henry O. Flipper becomes the first African American to graduate from West Point.
1914-1918	More than 400,000 African Americans serve in the U.S. armed forces during the First World War.

On May 15, two black soldiers, Henry Johnson and Needham Roberts become the first Americans to receive the French Medal of Honor (*croix de guerre*).	**1918**
In June, Benjamin O. Davis, Jr., graduates from West Point, the first black American to do so in the twentieth century.	**1936**
Benjamin O. Davis, Sr., becomes the first African-American general in the active Regular Army.	**1940**
American forces in World War II include more than a million African-American men and women.	**1941-1945**
On March 25, the Army Air Corps forms its first black unit, the 99th Pursuit Squadron.	**1941**
On August 24, Colonel Benjamin O. Davis, Jr., is made commander of the 99th Pursuit Squadron.	**1942**
On January 27 and 28, the airmen of the 99th Pursuit Squadron score a major victory against enemy fighters at the Italian seaside town of Anzio.	**1944**
On February 2, President Harry S Truman signs Executive Order 9981, ordering an end to segregation in the U.S. armed forces.	**1948**
Black and white forces fight side by side in Korea as separate black fighting units are disbanded.	**1950-1953**
Twenty African-American soldiers are awarded the Medal of Honor during the Vietnam War.	**1965-1973**
On April 28, Samuel L. Gravely becomes the first black admiral in the history of the U.S. Navy.	**1971**
In August, Daniel "Chappie" James becomes the first African American to achieve the rank of four-star general.	**1975**
On October 3, Colin Powell becomes the first African-American chairman of the Joint Chiefs of Staff.	**1989**
100,000 African-American men and women are sent to the Middle East during the Persian Gulf conflict.	**1990-1991**
On July 25, the Buffalo Soldier Monument is dedicated at Fort Leavenworth, Kansas.	**1992**

Index

References to photographs are listed in *italic, **boldface*** type.

Lear, Ben 36
Lewis, Walter 6–7, 42, 48, 51, 55
"Lonely Eagles" 32
Long, John D. 42, 44, 70

McConnell, E. G. *23*, 39, **73**
    at Camp Claiborne 30, 31, 35
    on General Patton 40–41
    on gunning 26–27, 37, 47
    on racism 23–24, 38
    Honskirch battle and 49–50
McNair, Leslie J. 21, 29
McNeil, Preston 17
Maginot Line 51
Miller, Dorie 20
Morville, Battle of 45, 47, 49

National Defense Training Act
    (1940) 15
99th Pursuit Squadron 32

103rd Infantry Division 59

Patton, George S. 7, 38, 40–41, **64,**
    65
Pearl Harbor attack (1941) 20
Presidential Unit Citation (PUC)
    11, 73–74, **75**

racial violence 32–34, *33*
racism (prejudice) 38, 48, 71–72
    at Camp Claiborne 30–31
    Eleanor Roosevelt and 18–19
    press and 67, 69
Randolph, A. Philip 14, 15–16, *19*
Rivers, Ruben 42, 43, 48, 65, *66*
Robinson, Jackie 25–26
Roosevelt, Eleanor 18–19, *19*
Roosevelt, Franklin D. 13, 14, 16,
    19, 20–21
Russian troops 63, 64

segregation 22–23, 30, 35. *See also*
    racism

of armed forces 14–15, 17, 18–
    19, 23–24, 31–32, 72
Selective Service Act, anti-
    discrimination clause of 14,
    17
Service Company 7, 34
17th Airborne Division 6, 57
71st Infantry Division 63
79th Infantry Division 58
784th Tank Battalion 22–25
758th Tank Battalion 22
Siegfried Line 59–62
Stevens, Johnnie 37, 41
    at Camp Claiborne 24
    at Camp Hood 35
    on gunning 58–59
    landing at Omaha Beach 38–39
    on segregation and racism 17,
    67, 69
    taking Hill 309 47–48
Stimson, Henry 15, 19

tanks *4*, *43*
    from A (Able) Company *46*
    General Sherman 26, 34, 39
    light 7, 34
Task Force Rhine 60–62
Tillet, Battle of 5–7, 53–57
Truman, Harry S 72
Turley, Samuel 45
26th Infantry Division 8, 40, 42,
    44, 51

White, Walter 14
Williams, David J. 66
    Battle of the Bulge and 51, 52
    Battle of Tillet and 5–7, 8, 54,
    55
    at Camp Claiborne 22–23
    racism and 25, 41–42
Women's Army Auxiliary Corps
    (WAACs) 70
Woodard, Isaac 71–72
World War I 12, 13

Bibliography

Anderson, Trezzvant W. *Come Out Fighting: The Epic Tale of the 761st Tank Battalion, 1942-1945.* Salzburger Druckerei Und Verlag, 1945.

Black, Wallace B., and Jean F. Blashfield. *Battle of the Bulge.* New York: Crestwood House, 1993.

Franklin, John Hope. *From Slavery to Freedom: A History of American Negroes.* New York: Alfred A. Knopf, 1966.

James, C.L.R., George Breitman, and Edgar Keemer. *Fighting Racism in World War II.* New York: Monad Press, 1980.

McGuire, Phillip. *Taps for a Jim Crow Army: Letters from Black Soldiers in World War II.* Santa Barbara, California: ABC-Clio, Inc., 1983.

Motley, Mary Penick, ed. *The Invisible Soldier.* Detroit: Wayne State University Press, 1975.

Nalty, Bernard C. *Strength for the Fight.* New York: The Free Press, A Division of Macmillan, Inc., 1986.

Potter, Lou, William Miles, and Nina Rosenblum. *Liberators: Fighting on Two Fronts in World War II.* New York: Harcourt Brace Jovanovich, Publishers, 1992.

Smith, Graham A. *When Jim Crow Met John Bull.* New York: St. Martin's Press, 1987.

Terkel, Studs. *"The Good War": An Oral History of World War Two.* New York: Pantheon Books, 1984.

Whiting, Charles. *Siegfried: The Nazis' Last Stand.* Briarcliff Manor, New York: Stein and Day, 1982.